101 Ways

to Clean Out the Clutter

Emilie Barnes

HARVEST HOUSE PUBLISHERS

EUGENE, OREGON

Cover by Dugan Design Group, Bloomington, Minnesota

101 WAYS TO CLEAN OUT THE CLUTTER
Copyright © 2008 by Emilie Barnes
Published by Harvest House Publishers
Eugene, Oregon 97402
www.harvesthousepublishers.com

Library of Congress Cataloging-in-Publication Data
    Barnes, Emilie.
    101 ways to clean out the clutter / Emilie Barnes.
        p. cm.
    ISBN-13: 978-0-7369-2263-0

    1. House cleaning. I. Title. II. Title: One hundred and one ways to clean out the clutter.
    TX324.C58 1997
    648'5—dc22

                                                                    2007028427

Printed in the United States of America

10 11 12 13 14 15 16 / BP-SK / 11 10 9

*Here, wherever it is, is your spot.
This place should be expressing something
of yourself. It should be communicating
something of you to your visitors, but it
should also satisfy something within you. You
should feel 'at home' here, because you have
made it home with something of yourself.*

EDITH SCHAEFFER

An Encouraging Word from Emilie

If you're like the women I meet, you long for a home without all the clutter that wears you out at the end of the day. Because so much of your time and energy are spent dusting, washing, waxing, and cleaning all your stuff, your husband, children, friends, and church may suffer.

With a little effort and a few helpful ideas, you can get control of all that stuff and learn to live how God intended—free to enjoy His creation. I believe this balanced life is already there in your heart. I hope that the ideas in this little book will help you shine forth as you de-clutter your home and embrace a life that is simply amazing.

Emilie Barnes

Why All That Clutter?

What is it about your lifestyle that causes you to be surrounded with clutter? Search your self, your habits, your routines, your methods, and even your philosophy about stuff to see what might lead to all that clutter.

I find that organized people have a calmness and serenity about them that disorganized people don't possess. Are you harried or distracted throughout much of your day? Does this unbalanced state of mind make your home and maybe even your work setting off kilter?

Pick an upcoming day to be extra aware of what triggers that sense of chaos or unrest. Is it a lack of communication, focus, or a schedule that does it? Consider how a different response to each trigger could shift you toward a more peaceful lifestyle.

No More Piles

Make sure everything has a designated place. One of my mottoes is, "Don't put it down, put it away." Another is, "Don't pile it, file it." If there is no place for stuff to go, it's going to be piled. Make it a goal to prevent those piles.

I know it isn't easy to do this at first, but soon you'll become hardwired to sift through mail, reports, statements, work, take-out menus, and whatever else is gathering on the counters and in the corners of your home. Either it is important enough to have a specific place or it's perfectly suited for the trash bin!

If going through papers, magazines, or bills initially feels overwhelming, choose a pile to take care of each day. Spend only five minutes sorting so you'll make quick decisions.

Remove the Unused

Get rid of all items you don't use. That means all clothes, furniture, bowls, cups, saucers, old records, old CDs, old videos, and so forth. It seems harmless to keep something around "just in case," but unused items take up valuable space. They also demand a significant portion of your time and attention when you handle, dust, wash, fold, and store them.

If you struggle to eliminate a shirt you haven't worn in three years, think how good it will feel to give it to a friend, a neighbor, a church, or a worthwhile organization.

Have you spent several rounds of "should I give this away" questioning on one particular item (or several)? That should be your cue to finally move it out the door. You'll feel lighter after you make these choices. Once you clear away a few items and experience the pleasure of uncluttering your life, you'll want to go back to the closets, the drawers, the corners, and the nooks to clear out even more.

Tools of the Trade

To be orderly you need proper tools: bins, hooks, racks, containers, file cabinets, file folders, and maybe a lazy Susan. Evaluate what you have on hand that can serve as a good paper holder, book shelf, or clothes hanger.

When organization is done right and suits your personal style, it will lead to simpler living. Give yourself the benefit of the ideal tool. Once you have a system in place that works, you won't have to keep deciding what to do with the piles.

Make a list of the tools you have and those you would like to purchase. Keep this with you so you can select the right materials when you are shopping— whether at garage sales, the Goodwill, or the local market.

It's a Family Matter

Involve the whole family. Learn to delegate jobs and responsibilities to other members of the family. Work with the children to de-clutter their bedrooms and bath. Dad can also be a big help, especially when you begin to clear out all the unused stuff in the garage.

Set a date for a cleaning bonanza and purchase all the cleaning supplies in advance. As a surprise for your family cleaning day, purchase a fun organizational tool for each family member—one that suits their individual personality. Or plan a relay cleaning day. Designate several projects that need to be done and assign a person to each task. Set a timer for 30 minutes and start working. When the buzzer sounds, each family member rotates to a different chore station. This plan keeps the energy high and nobody becomes bored.

Allow your family members to choose the background music for the work day and promise them pizza when everything is done. You could also reward the hard workers with a movie night and a walk-through tour to see how the rooms look with their makeover.

Labels Are Helpful

Use lots of labels and signs. If containers, bins, drawers, and shelves aren't labeled, the family won't be able to spot where things go. Use color coding to help identify items belonging to various members of the family; red bins for Christine, blue for Chad, and yellow for Bevan.

Keep your family involved in the process of simplifying the home life. You might be pleasantly surprised by how much they flourish in an uncluttered environment. Give your kids cleaning responsibilities at every age so that they get used to the benefits. Keep the tasks age-appropriate and be sure to acknowledge them for their efforts. Most of all, model the behavior yourself.

You will achieve grand dreams, a day at a time, so set goals for each day—not long and difficult projects, but chores that will take you, step by step, toward your rainbow. Write them down, if you must, but limit your list so that you won't have to drag today's undone matters into tomorrow. Remember that you cannot build your pyramid in twenty-four hours. Be patient. Never allow your day to become so cluttered that you neglect your most important goal—to do the best you can, enjoy this day, and rest satisfied with what you have accomplished.

OG MANDINO

A Place for Everything

Without too much detective work, we can figure out that most clutter happens because there isn't a set "home" for each item. Remember the old saying, "Everything has a place and everything is in its place." When everything has a place, you know where to find it, where to put it back, and you don't waste time searching through items to retrieve it.

Designate an easily accessible spot for your most used items. If those spots are filled with infrequently used items, clear them out and move them to storage (after you see if there is anything you can give away).

Choose a room and spend 30 minutes assigning a place for each item that fills the corners, clutters the surface areas, and blocks doorways.

To-Do Lists

Make a to-do list. List what you are going to do today to get rid of all your excess. It might include such things as:

- ☐ Discard all the old magazines on the coffee table.

- ☐ Have Weston go through his sock drawers and take out what he isn't using.

- ☐ Go through the refrigerator, including all containers and vegetable drawers, and toss out all expired and inedible foods. Reorganize each shelf.

- ☐ Start a compost pile in the backyard and put those vegetable leftovers to good use feeding your garden.

No More Excuses

Stop making excuses about why you keep all that clutter. Stop saying:

- ☐ Ugly $11.95 lamp: *I only bought it to change a $20 bill.*

- ☐ Leaky pans and buckets: *Someday I'll use them outdoors and put a plant in them.*

- ☐ Old sewing patterns: *I'm waiting until I have time to go through them.*

- ☐ An old sweater: *I paid good money for this.*

- ☐ Old Christmas cards: *Someday I'm going to use them for a decoupage picture.*

- ☐ An old platter: *I may need it someday.*

Do you recognize a few of these justifications? Eliminate the excuses and you'll make your life so much easier. Practice this today.

New Items In— Old Items Out

There is a great deal of wisdom in letting go of whatever chokes out the vitality in your life. When we're bogged down with too much of the old stuff, we don't make room for new ideas, fresh spaces, and creative living.

Try saying, "When something new comes in, something old must go." Now put it into practice. Next time you shop and make a purchase, try to think of what item you will discard when you get home. Believe me, this can be a great way to keep your spending in check and helps ease the potential build up of stuff. This rule is a huge help when you face a great sale. When you're standing in front of a sign that reads "Buy one, get one free," it's easy to load up without having a plan or place for anything you purchase that day. These items rarely find a permanent place in your home because you hadn't thought through their purpose or possibility—you just responded to the word "Sale!" Stick with the rule.

Unfinished Business

Do you ever feel like you're running in circles? Do you put off new pursuits because you are spending your precious time juggling projects that are never completed?

Make a list of five projects you would love to finish. Tackle these one at a time. You'll find that as you clear away the unfinished business, you'll be free to reach for new pursuits. Don't delay your goals and aspirations.

Which terminal projects are eating up the most time? Give yourself an absolute deadline to complete each one or consider letting go of the project altogether. Which projects are the most overwhelming and which have the highest priority? If you take care of a couple that are time sensitive, you'll give yourself breathing room and a sense of accomplishment. Consider the ones that absolutely must get done because others are counting on them or because they have a deadline. There's your starting place!

The 80/20 Rule

The 80/20 rule is one of the greatest principles you can use to figure out your top priorities. If all of the items on your to-do list are arranged in order of value, 80 percent of the value comes from only 20 percent of the items. The remaining 20 percent of the value comes from 80 percent of the items. Sometimes a little more and sometimes a little less.

The 80/20 rule suggests that in a list of ten projects, finishing two of them will yield 80 percent of the value. So don't be overwhelmed by a large list. Remember the top 20 percent of the list gives 80 percent of the value. What's left undone today can go on the list for tomorrow. Rearrange your to-do list so that it is in order of priority and keep the 80/20 rule in mind.

Accordion Files Fit the Bill

One item that makes great use of space and effort is an accordion file. Go to your local stationery store and purchase one or a few. Accordion files are wonderful and oh, so versatile. You can use them to store bills for future payment, to keep track of important papers, and to gather greeting and thank-you cards for those special occasions.

Set the files up with labels. For example, your bills folder could have pockets labeled "Pay," "Read," "Answer," "Pending," and "Hold." Designate a shelf for a row of accordion files. You'll be able to store many of your most needed paper items in these. And because accordion files are portable, you can take them with you to meetings so your records are handy or to the kitchen table when it's time to pay bills. Don't forget to purge them occasionally. The files won't serve you well if they are full of outdated or unneeded items.

As you simplify your life, the laws of the universe will be simpler; solitude will not be solitude, poverty will not be poverty, nor weakness.

HENRY DAVID THOREAU

The way we see the problem is the problem.

STEPHEN COVEY

Managing the Mail

Now, let's talk about the mail. The key to managing this area of our lives is doing it daily. If it can't be done when it arrives, assign a specific time each day to process it. One area of your home should be designated for this purpose—a desk, table, or a section of the kitchen counter. If you use the kitchen counter, be careful that it doesn't become a catchall area.

Remember the rule about paper: *Don't put it down, put it away.* It only takes a minute to sort the mail when it arrives, even if you can't process it at that moment. A simple file system can help you do this. You could use one file for letters you want to read. If you have older children, each might have his or her own folder to check when arriving home from school. There needs to be a file for bills, another for things you need to discuss with someone in the family, one for mail that needs to be answered, and maybe another for those that require a phone call.

Juggling the Junk Mail

Don't hesitate when junk mail and unwanted catalogs arrive. Don't worry about what you might be missing because the same items will be listed again in the next catalog—due to arrive in a couple of weeks. In fact, if you can get in the habit of instantly tossing junk mail, you'll get rid of at least 30 to 50 percent of your daily mail. When your favorite catalogs and magazines arrive, be sure to read them and then put them in the recycle bin or pass them along to a friend.

If you begin receiving too many catalogs and they are not ones that suit your lifestyle, call to cancel them and request that your name be removed from their mailing lists. Some catalogs are available online. You might consider receiving the email version of your favorite store's publication or an organization's email newsletter.

Break It Up

To accomplish a big task, break it into a few smaller parts—these become "instant tasks" that you can easily handle. It's the big items that throw us and leave us in a panic. Think of one project that you have put off because it seemed too big to take on after a busy day or in the middle of a hectic one.

For example, let's choose cleaning out the refrigerator as your dreaded project. Can you give it 15 minutes? Even the craziest of days usually have a few breaks in them that could be put to good use. Set a timer and work like mad for those 15 minutes evaluating leftovers, checking expiration dates, and wiping off shelves. Tomorrow, set the timer and toss out old vegetables, refresh the ice trays, and rinse the meat and produce bins. In a day or two you'll have invested two or three 15-minute sessions and completed the larger task of cleaning your refrigerator.

Practical Expectations

It's nice to want things done right, but not if you're crippled by the pressure. High expectations can lead to inactivity when you're overwhelmed. By all means do the best job you can do in a reasonable amount of time. However, don't get bogged down by perfectionism. You may know the difference in the finished product, but your friends and guests probably won't know or care if it's not perfectly done.

If you're preparing for guests, determine the cleaning that *must* be done versus the cleaning you *want* to get done. You'll find that if you clean the areas your guests will be visiting and just tidy other areas, you'll have a very welcoming environment. Always keep in mind that you want your home to be inviting, not sterile and immaculate. Aim for inviting rather than ideal, and you'll enjoy the time before and during your guests' visits. You'll be a much more sane hostess.

When Are You
Most Productive?

Each of us operates efficiently at different times of the day. Pay attention to when you feel the most energetic and alert. Take a few days to observe which time periods and what parts of each day are best for you when it comes to cleaning, working, juggling multiple tasks, focusing on one, and being creative. It might help to write out what you observe—it could be surprising. Maybe you always linger over breakfast and dishes to draw out the morning when it's actually your most energetic time and should tackle a couple work projects.

Don't use this awareness as an excuse to not perform well during your off period of the day. Instead, use it to be good to yourself and to enhance your life, productivity, sense of balance, and enjoyment. Schedule taxing chores for the hours when your mind is sharpest. Do the physical chores when you have the most energy. File papers or sweep the floor when you need a task that doesn't require too much thought and evaluation. This principle is good for work as well as at home.

Prevent Interruptions

M ost people are interrupted at least once every five minutes. If this is true for you, analyze what's causing those interruptions. You and your situation are unique—the things that disrupt your day are different than the things that disrupt another's day. If you haven't studied this loss of time, become aware of it. You will be amazed at how much time is whittled away by these interruptions and disturbances.

Consider how to safeguard your time. There's nothing wrong with telling people you can see them at 9:30, 12:15, or 6:40 exactly. Even family members can be taught not to interrupt. Maybe you cause the interruptions by insisting on checking email every few minutes or answering your cell phone even when you are in the middle of something. If you don't respect your time, others certainly won't know how to respect your time.

Today Is the Day!

Resolve to make each and every day count. Instead of constantly anticipating tomorrow, live for today. When you invest in tomorrow's worries or schedule, you're missing out on what is supposed to happen or be experienced today! Have you ever spent a great deal of time fretting over a future obligation or task only to find that it was not that burdensome— but the weeks of worrying were?

Make today count toward your pursuit of a more organized life. Select one item and find an ideal place for it. Now, when that item ends up on the coffee table or on the kitchen counter, you'll know exactly where it belongs. Your quest to de-clutter your home can truly be this simple.

We do not keep the outward form of order,
where there is deep disorder in the mind.

WILLIAM SHAKESPEARE

It is best to do things systematically,
since we are only human, and
disorder is our worst enemy.

HESIOD (800 BC)

The Family Communication Center

Hang a bulletin board, pegboard, racks, or other wall-mounted storage where it can be seen by all members of your family. This will become your home "communication center." Messages can be sent, messages can be received, and messages can be displayed here. Other helpful supplies to keep in this area include a dry erase board, a calendar, a list of important phone numbers, and a key holder. Encourage your family to use this area by leaving special notes or treats for them to pick up every now and then.

This center is really helpful to have in place when babysitters and houseguests are over. Be sure to write a nice greeting on the white board for your guests, or pin a greeting card and their guest keys to the bulletin board.

Purge the Paper Piles

Get rid of extra paper. Almost 90 percent of all paper in your home and office is never referred to again. That's a staggering amount of paper! Choose a room, any room, and there is probably a pile of paper stashed in a drawer, cupboard, or even loose on furniture surfaces. In the kitchen you might have recipes, cooking articles, and grocery lists piling up. In your office school papers, bills, and receipts gather. Your bedroom ends up being a place for scraps of reminder notes and magazines to accumulate.

Pick a room and go straight for the papers. Allow yourself to keep only a few pieces, maybe five, and toss the rest. Yes, you can keep more if they are important. However, if it's a piece you haven't referred to in a while, won't need anymore, or mean to read but never will…it goes. Toss at least ten times the amount of stuff you keep. Your rooms will look and feel so much better—and so will you.

Smart Storage Solutions

Sometimes all it takes to eliminate mess, clutter, and confusion are a few hooks here, a basket or two there, and reshuffling items on a shelf. Take a look around your house. Do you have trunks, chests, or baskets that could be used for storage? All of these can look quite lovely in a room while storing blankets, books, DVDs, and other items. If the piece is large like a trunk and mainly serves as a table or TV stand, then only store items in it that you don't need regularly, such as heavy blankets or seasonal decorations.

Take a look at where the most clutter gathers in your home. Then see if one of the storage pieces you already have could ease the mess. If not, measure the area or wall space and go visit one of those great stores that specializes in storage units. With only a few key pieces, you can reform most any cluttered corner. The storage store will also give you ideas for using the baskets, boxes, and chests that you already have.

Filing Financials

Many banks offer bill-paying services to their customers. You can use your computer to communicate with the bank. Each bank has its own format and the remote services are usually easy to set up for home use. This little helper will free you up from having to spend time writing and mailing all your bill payments each month.

How much of your paper pile up is related to financial records? It's amazing how many bank statements, reports, and paycheck stubs end up in the bedroom or on the kitchen table instead of in a file drawer in a home office or office area! If you don't know what to save or shred, learn what to keep and where to keep it. Separate "permanent" records from "current" records and place permanent documents in a safe-deposit box. File the current records at home using a file system that makes sense to you. Be sure to tell someone where you store your records.

Commit to record-keeping each week. There. It really can be that simple. Weekly maintenance is easier than a complete overhaul once a year!

Get Motivated!

Your attitude is one of the most useful tools available in your desire to clean out what is cluttered and make a difference in your home or work environment. This is especially true if one of your biggest obstacles is lack of motivation. If you look around and see a mess or a setting that doesn't suit your lifestyle, taste, or your family's growing needs, don't be discouraged. And don't let laziness or lack of motivation stop you from making a change for the better. "Lazy people want much but get little, while the diligent are prospering" (Proverbs 13:4 TLB).

Be one of the diligent, one of the prosperous ones. Turn your negative attitude into an internal dialogue that is encouraging, supportive, and energetic. Start your day by congratulating yourself on the effort you made the day before. Look at the cupboard you organized or the corner you finally cleared of shoes and baseball caps. Celebrate the small steps—your attitude will continue to inspire more and more effort.

Stick a Label On It

There are many uses for those little printed address labels. Stick one on an item before loaning it out. Put one on your camera and each of your tools. Use them to label items you've left for repair.

Blank labels are very useful too. Mark blank labels to identify boxes full of seasonal clothing or your children's outgrown clothing you want to save for their siblings or other family members.

In the kitchen, use labels to keep track of which jars or plastic containers hold flour, salt, sugar, and cereals. If you have the task of making lunches for several children, use labels on each of their plastic sandwich containers and water bottles.

An office becomes more efficient and simplified when you label notebook spines, file folders, drawers, and shelf sections to indicate the type of books or office supplies stored there.

Tips to Tackle the Garage

Dad can be a big help when it comes to de-cluttering the garage. Remember, garages are built to park cars in, not to store all your excess. Here are a few tips to help in this area:

- ☐ Throw away paint and oil stained rags or store them in a metal container.

- ☐ Dispose of combustibles such as newspapers, magazines, boxes, and old furniture.

- ☐ Install extra lighting in work areas, especially where power tools are used.

- ☐ Make sure ladders are sturdy and have nonslip tread on the rungs.

- ☐ Power tools should have double insulation or grounded plugs.

- ☐ Make sure all aisles are clear of debris to prevent accidents.

Organizing is sustainable, if your system is built around the way you think and designed to grow and adapt with you as your life and work change. It is when your system is a poor fit for you that maintenance is a difficult chore.

JULIE MORGENSTERN,
ORGANIZING FROM THE INSIDE OUT

For the most part, we, who could choose simplicity, choose complication.

ANNE MORROW LINDBERGH,
GIFT FROM THE SEA

The Drop-off
And Pick-up Place

Identify a drop-off spot for items in transit—those things you are supposed to take to work or school tomorrow. Almost everyday you likely have items that you or one of your family members need to take somewhere. But in the morning rush, it is so easy to forget what seemed so important the night before. Designate a consistent spot where you can set library books, dry cleaning, mail, borrowed items that need to be returned to neighbors or friends, backpacks, briefcases, spare shoes, homework, a signed note for a field trip, or your gym clothes.

If you don't have a large entryway or logical corner, use a trunk, a set of shelves, or a large basket that can hold the most common items. A few hooks placed above your storage bin can hold clothing items. A brightly colored folder is ideal for permission slips, library cards, or bus passes. Your mornings will be so much more enjoyable.

No More Lost Keys

Reduce time spent looking for misplaced items. Hang tiny hooks or a low shelf next to the pegboard rack to organize keys, sunglasses, garage door openers, and other easily misplaced items.

We are back, once again, to finding a proper spot for everything. See how important it is? Consider which items you are constantly searching for and then determine the most convenient location to store them. The location that is easiest to stick with is the one closest to your point of entry. As soon as you come into the house, you should have a place for those crucial items so that you won't be tempted to carry them into the kitchen or set them on top of the television.

Most families benefit from having this collection spot near their front door, but if you and your family members tend to come into the house from the garage—that's the place to put it.

A Tote for Household Tools

Buy a toolbox or a fishing tackle box to hold your tools rather than trust them to the jumble of a kitchen drawer or an already overcrowded shelf in the garage. We use basic tools quite frequently around our house. Hammers, wrenches, and small screwdrivers always have a purpose in a busy household. They also disappear. They scatter to all corners of the house—wherever the last project took place. However, if all the tools are kept together in a portable box, they can easily be carried to the next project. And once the task is complete, it's easy to return this box to its proper place in the garage, pantry, or wherever you decide it belongs.

Have fun selecting this toolbox. If you have kids, let them choose a brightly colored container or bring home a plain one and let them decorate it with stickers, paint, and labels.

Phone Calls Take Time Too

Learn how to cut off time-consuming calls without hurting feelings. It's okay to say, "This is a bad time for me. May I call you back?" Or talk briefly and then tell them, "It's good to talk with you. Thanks for calling," and say goodbye. There will be times when you need to give a person undivided attention on the phone, but most calls are simply about daily tasks, schedules, and requests.

It's important to set boundaries about when you will answer phone calls and how long you'll talk. How many times have you planned a project for the day and then let one phone call stop your momentum? It's easy to say "yes" to a conversation or to a friend's suggestion to go to lunch and say "no" to cleaning the hall closet, paying the bills, or completing a work project. Don't let the temptation undermine your personal motivation!

Let calls go to voicemail during certain hours so that you control when and where you respond. Learn to say "no" until you've completed what you've set out to do. Sometimes this involves saying "no" to yourself!

Don't Delay Small Tasks

Do small chores as needed so they occupy the least amount of time possible. Put a shirt back on the hanger, repair the sag on the rear gate, replace that burned-out light bulb, and put new batteries in your smoke alarm. If you start taking care of the immediate tasks rather than save them for later, you'll notice an amazing difference in your clutter problem. The small stuff adds up to big projects later—don't let them snowball.

As you go about your day today, pay attention to which tasks can be done immediately. The dishwasher can be loaded, the cereal box can be put in the cupboard, the dining table can be cleared so that it's clean for dinner, and your paid bills can be filed. Things are looking better already!

Be My Guest

Be a guest in your own home for a day. If you walk into your living room, what stands out? What looks messy? Inviting? Fun? This fresh inventory of your living room and each room in your house will awaken you to ways to clean out and cheer up your home. I'd encourage you to have fun with this. Do one room at a time and take a few notes about this "first impression" makeover. Then get ready to make a difference in that room.

What's working? What's pleasing? What draws your eye? Look for items that just don't fit. Most importantly decide the focal point for your room. What do you want people to see when they enter the room? The focal point is the anchor—the center of gravity. Find that and you're well on your way! Not a bad idea for every area of your life.

Little Tasks Take Little Time

Few of us have several hours to clean out our closets. The key is to use the ten-minute segments you do have to accomplish a small task or make a dent in a larger one. For example:

- ☐ clean one shelf in your closet
- ☐ make an appointment with the dentist
- ☐ put in a load of wash
- ☐ make out your shopping list
- ☐ answer a few emails

You'll de-clutter if you learn to do small tasks in small blocks of time. Try recording reminders by using a small recorder while putting on your makeup or waiting for the bus.

The sculptor produces the beautiful statue by chipping away such parts of the marble block as are not needed— it is a process of elimination.

ELBERT HUBBARD

We don't need to increase our goods nearly as much as we need to scale down our wants. Not wanting something is as good as possessing it.

DONALD HORBAN

Just Give It a Try

Is your accumulation of stuff what drew you to this book? I can relate. Most women can. What many people don't realize is how incredibly freeing it is to get rid of clutter. They just see the work involved, the logistics, the possible changes, and the future commitment to keeping a home clean. They can't envision the openness, the beauty, and the peace this change will offer them and their families.

Keep your eye on the prize—the sanctuary you will create when you remove the obstacles of clutter. If you're new to this or hesitant to begin, don't look at your house as a whole. Start with one room. If you incorporate just a few of the suggestions in this book or ones you've gathered from magazines, you'll see transformation. The results of your one room makeover will give you the energy and the desire to keep life simple and lovely.

A Chance to Change

It's time to stop rationalizing why we keep all of the junk in our homes. In order to say "I don't need that anymore," you have to get organized from the inside out. Maybe you like stuff around you because you had chaos around you as a child. Or maybe the clutter on the outside reflects how jumbled up you feel in your heart and mind.

Give yourself the very wonderful gift of change. Even if this scares you a little bit...keep moving forward. You'll see great results. As you work toward making your home a refuge and a sanctuary, you'll notice how much more calm you feel inside. It works the other way too. If you take time to pray, be silent, and become peaceful in your heart, you'll want your surroundings to match.

Do You Really Need It?

Our old habits of buying unneeded stuff must be conquered. Advertisements, stores, and even friends and neighbors tell you that you need this and you need that! But those who want to simplify and live life in rich ways have to stand up and be counted—you really don't need that.

De-cluttering is simply stating "I don't need that" as you go from room to room. When this becomes your fight song, it makes it so much easier to cut back on all the excess that causes clutter. Try it in a room today. Look at that collection of baskets you have that gathers more dust than compliments. Sort through them as you repeat your new song of simplicity. Yes, keep a couple, but be sure you keep ones that are truly useful and get rid of the umpteen ones that are not. Go to your clothes closet. Ask yourself, "What haven't I worn in months?" Why hang on to something that needs to be hung up in an already full closet?

Sell? Donate? Toss Out?

Uncluttering your home doesn't mean that you throw everything in the trash. In fact there are several other good alternatives. Here are a few:

- ☐ have a garage sale
- ☐ donate items to a worthy organization that helps the needy
- ☐ donate to your church's needs
- ☐ give to needy friends you know
- ☐ package items up and send useful ones to a missionary supported by your church
- ☐ advertise on eBay

The items you don't need could be the items others are hoping to have and use. The best form of recycling turns a waste of space into an opportunity, a blessing, or a gift for another person. Start giving.

Breaking Down
the Big Ones

Don't look at the whole mess, but break the big tasks down into smaller tasks. That way you aren't overwhelmed with what you see. Psychologically, a small part is easier to assimilate than the whole. For example, start with one room at a time. Then focus on one corner at a time. Look at small projects within that area.

The most blatant projects are often the "procrastination piles"—the items, papers, or projects that accumulate in corners and on dressers, chairs, or any surface area for that matter! You intend to get to these eventually so you leave them out in the open, but soon they are not visual reminders—only eye sores. Tackle these. Decide which projects should still happen, which could be tossed, which are outdated, and which could be delegated. Small steps will transform your home in big ways.

The Paper Shuffle

One of the most difficult tasks to manage is cleaning up all the paper that comes into your home. How you handle that in an efficient manner will depend on how hung up you are on handling all this paper more than once. The fewer times you handle paper, the more efficient your system is. The ultimate goal is to handle each piece just one time. Try to determine whether that paper is necessary or not needed the moment you pick it up. Then, either put it in its proper place or dispose of it.

The papers that fill your home right now have probably been handled numerous times. Do you notice how they rarely get to their final resting place? Pursue this new goal with conviction. It can take extra time in the beginning, but in the end it will give you a clutter-free existence.

Distributing the Mail

Incoming mail is a good test case. When mail arrives, immediately begin the process of distributing it. As you touch each item decide:

- ☐ *Is it junk?* Toss in the trash. This usually eliminates at least 50 percent of the mail.

- ☐ *To whom does it belong?* If it is a bill, give it to the person in the family who is responsible for paying bills.

- ☐ *Does it need follow-up?* Give it to the member of the family who will take care of it. (Respond within 48 hours.)

- ☐ *Does it require reading?* Place it in your reading file folder so you can read it at your leisure, while waiting at the doctor's office or while waiting to pick up your children at one of their events.

The art of progress is to preserve order amid change.

ALFRED NORTH WHITEHEAD

We all know that if you don't fertilize the soil before you plant a garden, nothing can grow. If you don't knock down the old house and haul away the debris, it's impossible to lay a new foundation and build a house. We have all heard it said a thousand times before: You have to get rid of the old to make room for the new.

DEBBIE FORD, *THE BEST YEAR OF YOUR LIFE*

Filing the Files

What does one do with all the paper that needs to be filed away for record keeping? Many people prefer to file their papers in file folders and store the folders in file drawers, boxes, baskets, or other containers. Be sure to label the containers and manila file folders using the following basic headings:

- ☐ auto
- ☐ bank statements
- ☐ credit cards
- ☐ escrow papers
- ☐ insurance
- ☐ Internal Revenue Service
- ☐ medical
- ☐ Social Security

If you're practicing the rule to handle each piece of paper just once, this system will help make that a reality. If you have a place for each piece of paper, you won't need all those in-between spots.

Evening…
a Time to Clean Up

Get your children and husband into the habit of cleaning up after themselves, especially before bedtime. Schedule a family meeting to explain the new routine and get everybody on board. Initially they might not be too excited about the idea of an evening clean up session, but you can make developing this new habit fun. Stress the importance of waking up to an orderly home and ask everyone for ideas so each member is included in the pursuit of this new goal.

It takes 21 days to form a new habit so don't be discouraged on day 12 if they haven't caught the vision! Press on. Keep the cleaning simple. You can either set a certain amount of time each person needs to spend cleaning or designate an area for them to maintain. Even little kids can clean their rooms in just a few minutes. Adjust the cleaning plan as you go so that it works best for your family.

Beware of Procrastination and Laziness

Procrastination is one of the main reasons we don't de-clutter our homes—and laziness is one reason a person procrastinates. The book of Proverbs speaks about this poor character trait:

☐ As a door turns on its hinges, so a sluggard turns on his bed (verse 26:14).

☐ Do not love sleep or you will grow poor; stay awake and you will have food to spare (verse 20:13).

☐ One who is slack in his work is brother to one who destroys (verse 18:9).

So get out of bed, put your feet on the floor, and start out your day with a purpose. Don't be a sluggard when it comes to uncluttering your home. Put action to your desires!

Why So Many?

In most cases we don't need more than one of anything. As you survey all your stuff, you will soon discover that you have multiple screwdrivers, spoons, glasses, tape measures, flashlights, pliers, boxes of cereal, and cans of pasta mix.

Why do you hang on to all these multiples? Perhaps you think that if you have more than one, you have a better chance of finding it when you want it. Multiple things take up a lot of space in an already cluttered area. Here are two suggestions that might help you find that one of a kind object (whatever it might be):

☐ Decide on an exact place to put it.

☐ Always return it to that spot the minute you are through using it. Is this rule sinking in yet?

Clear the Clutter
in Child's Room

Children's rooms also need the proper tools and equipment in order to keep from accumulating a lot of clutter. Consider these suggestions:

- ☐ Keep a small vacuum handy to quickly clean up messes.

- ☐ Put up a blackboard to write on or a peg-board to hang things on to keep things off the floor.

- ☐ Use extra large wastebaskets with plastic garbage can liners.

- ☐ Organize toys in plastic boxes, milk crates, or decorated cartons.

- ☐ Install closet rods (appropriate to the height of the children) so they can hang up their own clothes.

- ☐ Limit snacking in bedrooms.

The Closet of Mystery

All of us have "ghostly closets." They are a mystery even to us. We open the doors just to see what we have stuffed into them.

As a child I can remember listening to one of my all-time favorite radio programs, *Fibber McGee and Molly*. During one of those episodes, Molly opened up her closet and everything tumbled out of it—many things that didn't even belong there. But because it was behind closet doors, no one except Molly could see into the closet.

If you have one of those mystery closets, begin today to get a grip on it. Take everything out, lay the items on the floor or bed, and examine each item to see if it still fits or if you've worn it in the last year. It must pass your inspection before you put it back into the closet. If the item doesn't pass the test, you must give it away or put it into the garage sale bag.

The Messy Medicine Cabinet

When you open your medicine cabinet, do you feel as though you've just walked into the Rite Aid Pharmacy? Do you have one of every pill prescribed by mankind? Have some of the items expired three years ago? Do you find old toothbrushes and half-filled tubes of toothpaste? Do you have old ointments, tweezers, eye makeup, and nail polishes of various shades of red and purple?

If so then you need a "medicine chest makeover." Attack with vigor—get rid of all that old stuff you no longer use. Make sure you don't throw out old medicines in a way that children could mistakenly find them. Don't use your easy-to-reach medicine cabinet to store all of your feminine items. Be selective about what you keep in this handy storage spot.

Cleanliness and order are not matters of instinct; they are matters of education, and like most great things, you must cultivate a taste for them.

BENJAMIN DISRAELI

Order is not pressure which is imposed on society from without, but an equilibrium which is set up from within.

JOSE ORTEGA Y GASSET

Broken and Outgrown Toys

Do you suffer from kiddie clutter in your home? As I visit homes where children live, I'm amazed at how many toys, games, gadgets, puzzles, and books there are in the home. You know who is responsible for much of this clutter? Parents and grandparents— not the kids!

In many cases these toys are missing parts and the games are no longer played with (because they are for three- to five-year-olds and the child is now nine). Take an inventory of all this clutter. Set aside those items that should be given away, tossed out, or added to the garage sale bag.

As long as you keep all of this kid stuff clutter, you are having to store it, dust it, move it, and spend your energy vacuuming around it. This is a de-clutter paradise. Check to make sure that your children have shelves, closets, baskets, and trunks to store their belongings. If they don't have proper places to store their toys, everything will end up strewn across the floor, or in piles at the bottom of their closets.

Do the Worst First

One of the basic principles I share in my organizational seminars is "do the worst first." Once you complete the worst part of the project, everything else is easy. This is also a great rule to follow if you have trouble with procrastinating. We all dread the worst—that's why it is best to get it out of the way in the beginning of the project.

When you enter a room with plans to clean it, determine which of the projects you dread most. Take a minute to break down the whole job into smaller tasks. Now choose the worst of the small tasks and do that one first. You will learn two things about this "do the worst first" rule:

☐ It didn't take you as long as you thought.

☐ It wasn't as bad as you thought it would be.

Friends Help Friends

Working with a friend is always more fun than working alone. Try calling a friend to see if you can help her for a day at her home in exchange for her helping you for a day in your home. A day is just a figure of speech. It might mean helping each other for just two hours—the idea is to help each other out. When you have a friend helping you, you'll discover several things:

- ☐ It's more fun.
- ☐ The job is completed faster.
- ☐ They will help you decide what to keep and what to eliminate.
- ☐ They will hold you accountable to continue with your project.

When you set up the exchange with your friend, be sure to allow enough time to break for a cup of tea and some sweet bread. That's a reward to look forward to.

Learn to Let Go

Do you have difficulty letting go of material possessions you no longer love or use? These old possessions take up a lot of wasted space in your home. Try this. Pretend that you've just sold your home and need to pack what you will be taking to your new home. You are moving across the country and you have to weigh each item's value against the cost of moving things you no longer need. Ask yourself these questions:

- ☐ Is it worth the cost of moving it?
- ☐ Is this item worth the time and effort it will take to pack and move it?
- ☐ Do you have the energy to carry it out to the moving van?
- ☐ Is it worth the time and energy it will take to unwrap it at the new home?
- ☐ Will you have a place for it at the new house or will it just take up precious space?

If you answer "no" to most of these questions, you might want to find a new home for the object.

The Proverbs 31 Woman

A wife of noble character who can find?
She is worth far more than rubies.
Her husband has full confidence in her
and lacks nothing of value.
She brings him good, not harm,
all the days of her life.
She selects wool and flax
and works with eager hands.
She is like the merchant ships,
bringing her food from afar.
She gets up while it is still dark;
she provides food for her family
and portions for her servant girls.
She considers a field and buys it;
out of her earnings she plants a vineyard.
She sets about her work vigorously;
her arms are strong for her tasks.
She sees that her trading is profitable,
and her lamp does not go out at night.
In her hand she holds the distaff
and grasps the spindle with her fingers.

She opens her arms to the poor
and extends her hands to the needy.
When it snows, she has no fear for her household;
for all of them are clothed in scarlet.
She makes coverings for her bed;
she is clothed in fine linen and purple.
Her husband is respected at the city gate,
where he takes his seat among the elders of the land.
She makes linen garments and sells them,
and supplies the merchants with sashes.
She is clothed with strength and dignity;
she can laugh at the days to come.
She speaks with wisdom,
and faithful instruction is on her tongue.
She watches over the affairs of her household
and does not eat the bread of idleness.
Her children arise and call her blessed;
her husband also, and he praises her:
"Many women do noble things, but you surpass them all."
Charm is deceptive, and beauty is fleeting;
but a woman who fears the Lord is to be praised.
Give her the reward she has earned,
and let her works bring her praise at the city gate.

Hydrogen Peroxide Has Many Uses

One of the great de-clutter tools you should always have on hand is a bottle of hydrogen peroxide 3%. Use it to do the following:

☐ Disinfect bathrooms. Fill a spray bottle with a 50/50 mixture of peroxide and water and keep it in every bathroom to disinfect without harming your septic system like bleach will.

☐ Add a cup of peroxide (instead of bleach) to a load of whites—this will whiten them.

☐ Use it as a vegetable wash to kill bacteria and neutralize chemicals.

☐ Clean and disinfect your dishwasher, refrigerator, counters, and tabletops.

Shopping Tips

After you've gone through your wardrobe and removed the clothes you haven't worn for at least a year or those that no longer fit, you might need to replace a few items. Keep these ideas in mind when you go shopping:

☐ Shop early in the day for best merchandise selection.

☐ Check out the special clearance racks.

☐ Don't buy something just because it's a bargain.

☐ Always check the care labels. "Dry clean only" items can end up costing you more money than you save on the sale price.

☐ Carefully examine the irregulars and seconds for rips or stains.

☐ Only purchase pieces that work with several outfits.

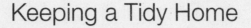

Keeping a Tidy Home

Many times clutter happens because we lack certain tools to bunch those loose items together. You might find these ideas helpful as you try to clean up and organize the various areas of your home:

- ☐ Keep the floors of your closets clear so you can vacuum them without having to move a lot of stuff.

- ☐ Make sure a wastebasket and laundry bin are placed in every bedroom.

- ☐ Hang a peg rack in a few rooms or closets. Be sure there are enough clothes hangers in each closet.

- ☐ Place a decorative bowl on top of each dresser to put loose coins and pocket items in.

- ☐ Hang clothes organizers on the back of doors.

- ☐ Install additional shelving in your closets.

*Three Rules of Work: Out of clutter find
simplicity; From discord find harmony; In
the middle of difficulty lies opportunity.*

ALBERT EINSTEIN

*The best and safest thing is to keep a balance
in your life, acknowledge the great powers
around us and in us. If you can do that, and
live that way, you are really a wise man.*

EURIPIDES

Store Items Where Needed

A lot of things become clutter only because they aren't kept where you need them most. Store things according to where you use them. Don't store coffee away from the coffeemaker or linens in a cupboard in the garage. Things need to be stored near like things. You'll find that many items will be used if they are moved to a more logical storage location.

Keep track of how often you travel from place to place or room to room in order to accomplish a task. If this happens quite a lot, time and energy is being wasted, and it's clear that you don't quite have things where they belong. If your hall closet is overflowing with cleaning supplies that tumble out every time you retrieve a towel, take those supplies out of the closet and place them in the rooms where you use them. This frees up your hall closet and makes cleaning your kitchen or bathroom a faster task. If your kitchen drawer is stocked with extra pens, paper, and paperclips, move those items to the office or the area where you keep your bills and files.

Be a Good Steward

Look at items you typically throw away. Can they be used again, either once or multiple times? This might seem like a way to gather clutter, but if you are wise in your choices, you end up with useful items around you. And if you reuse items in cool, functional ways, you will cut down on how much you spend and how much you acquire when you go shopping. It's all about being a good steward of what you have, what you bring in, and what you release. When you are a good steward, de-cluttering your life and home become much easier.

For example, save the plastic trays that come with store bought cookies and pastries. After dividing large quantities of fresh meat into family serving sizes, set each portion on a tray and slip it into a freezer bag. It will slide in very easily. When it comes time to defrost the meat, slide the tray out of the freezer bag. The tray holds the juices until the meat is defrosted.

Find Another Use

We all make purchase mistakes. Food our family won't touch. A movie or game that everyone ignores. The latest brand or color of makeup. You name it, we'll try it—right? But that isn't always the secret to success. Be thankful for the brands you love and trust no matter what. However, when you venture out, try a new product, and discover you don't like it, don't waste the new item. Find another use for it.

Don't throw out sample size shampoos or those you tried and didn't like. Instead, use them to wash your combs and brushes. Shampoos are specially formulated to remove oils from your hair—they work equally well on those same oils on your combs and brushes.

You could also pass that new, unwanted product along to a friend. Chances are she was just thinking about trying that very same shampoo, workout DVD, book, or cereal.

Simple Ideas
Make Easier Days

What items or habits might make your days simpler? Buy a 30-foot heavy-duty extension cord for the vacuum cleaner. It enables you to clean the entire hallway and staircase without unplugging the cord. Make life easier on yourself with extras like the long cord.

Those handheld vacuum units are nice to have in the family room or the kitchen for quick cleanups. A large, handled basket placed at the foot of the stairs can be used to collect a day's worth of books, socks, and shoes. At the end of the day, use the basket to pack everything back up the stairs. Save time by keeping your favorite multipurpose cleanser in each bathroom and the kitchen —this might even inspire another member of the household to clean these areas. When you make one of your family's favorite dishes, create a large batch and freeze enough for one or two more dinners. The next time you enjoy this meal, you won't have the clutter that comes with the cooking!

Unused Electric Gadgets

Just because it is electrical doesn't mean you have to own it. How many times do you use your electric scissors, electric card shufflers, electric carving knives, or electric bottle warmers? Just because something has an electric cord doesn't mean you have to have it taking up space in your home. There's nothing wrong with doing things the old manual way. Get those seldom used electrical gadgets off your shelves and put them on your garage sale table.

Once you get rid of these items, you won't have to ever charge them again or keep their sometimes uniquely sized batteries on hand. The electric items listed above would take up a couple drawers or entire cupboard shelf. The manual versions would require only part of a drawer or no space at all!

Watch for Hidden Costs

In junk mathematics we see that junk causes more junk. When you get a new cookbook, you have to then buy a plastic cookbook holder so you can read the book easier and shield it from drips and splatters. This holder takes up counter space and must be washed and dried periodically. So when you buy an item, be aware of what you'll have to purchase to accommodate the item.

What can you see around your house that seemed like a good idea at the time, but came with too many accessories or add-ons? I'm sure that more than a few parents look at the tangle of cords, stacks of games, and multiple remotes in their family room and question why they ever bought video game units as Christmas gifts!

Plasticware Everywhere

Look into the cupboard or on the shelves that hold all your plastic containers. You probably have many items that don't have lids, or you have lids that don't have the matching containers. How many of these plastic pieces do you really need? Take them all out of storage and go through them to match the bottoms with their lids. If you don't have a match, toss the mismatch away. Then survey what's left. Just how many quart size containers do you need? If you have too many duplicates, you need to give them away or put them in your garage sale bag.

Those extra plastic lids can come in handy when you're moving furniture. Slip them under the legs of heavy furniture and it will be much easier to slide the furniture around a carpeted room. When finished throw them in the recycle bin!

Life is too complicated not to be orderly.

MARTHA STEWART

*The feeling went beyond everyday cleanliness
and order. The air felt alive, almost vibrating.
Can a room have a heartbeat? Can space
be serene and exciting at the same time? I'd
never been in a room that felt like that.*

SUE BENDER, *PLAIN AND SIMPLE*

Paper Bags, Newspapers, Bottles, and Cans

Have you ever seen a brown paper bag you didn't like or didn't keep? Stack after stack of brown bags are in garages across America because we think that someday we'll find a reason to use them. Don't feel guilty about getting rid of all those bags. After all, they are biodegradable and will break down in our landfills. And you're always able to collect them faster than you can use them.

Check to see what else is piling up in your garage. Cans and bottles you keep meaning to take in to the recycle center for refunds. Newspapers. Months and months worth of newspapers. Surplus supplies that you stock up on because you are a wise shopper. (But how many extra packages of toilet paper do you need?) Do you have piles of formerly used sports equipment, toys or carpet remnants from a project two years ago? The garage could use a touch of de-cluttering.

Freezer Food Fuss

Do you keep moving that cut of meat in the freezer because you can't think of a recipe to use to prepare it? Do you just keep shifting it from the lower shelf in your freezer to the top shelf and back again to the bottom shelf? Don't hold on to an item until it gets a freezer burn and you have to throw it away. Make a pact with yourself that you won't bring any more food into the freezer until you use up what's already there.

While you're in the kitchen, take inventory of your pantry and cupboards to determine what items never get used and which ones are always being restocked. Keep this information in mind or on a list so that you can streamline your next trip to the grocery store. And remember—no more pounds of hamburger until you use the one you've been shuffling around that freezer for weeks.

Use It or Lose It

We all have that basket or drawer full of free items that we have accumulated over the years: hand lotions, shampoos, conditioners, soaps, perfumes, and so forth. Either start using them or toss them out. This kind of purging can take place all over the house.

It's time for a quiz! Give yourself one point every time you answer yes. Do you have enough space? Are things piling up in the closet? Are there stacks of unread magazines sitting around? Do certain items constantly get lost? Are things collecting on the top of your refrigerator? Are you finding stuff you haven't used in over a year? Are you buying things you already have—because you can't find them?

If you score zero to three, pretty good! If you score four to six, you could definitely use some improvement! Set aside one hour this week to think through solutions for these problem areas. Try to do this next month too.

Share Your Heirlooms Now

What things do you treasure? A delicate set of dishes. An afghan from your grandmother. A child's drawing. A watch. These are all treasures of the heart and home. They inspire sweet memories. Go through your storage boxes, old photos, even your grandmother's Bible. Begin sharing these things with your children or grandchildren. Dust off the old scrapbook and bring out the quilt you love.

Beautiful table linens from your mom, grandmother, or great-grandmother are well worth preserving. Because folding textiles weakens the fabric, loosely roll linens, lace, and other delicate fabrics onto cardboard tubes. The tubes used for mailing posters are available in most office supply stores. You will be happy to learn that rolled items require little or no ironing so they are always ready when you want to serve a special meal, set a pretty table, or plan a celebration. By sharing your heirlooms, you stop cluttering up your drawers and start filling your life with the treasures of a family.

Use Up the Leftovers

Get rid of clutter by doing something with your leftovers. And I don't mean food. I mean your bits and pieces of stuff that can do double-duty! Use wallpaper pieces as gift wrap. Leftover paint can be used to touch up a thrift-store find or scratched baseboards. Don't waste anything. It's amazing what you can do with leftovers!

What else do you have right under your nose that could be a perfect find? Go on a scavenger hunt in your own home. Better yet, involve your family in the quest to find something old that could be turned into something new. As they point out items that haven't been used in awhile, you can all vote whether or not to transform it or trash it! The only limit is your ability to think creatively.

Speed Cleaning

Enter a new sport—speed cleaning. Here are some tips to make it all happen quickly and efficiently. (1) Start at the top of a room and work your way down and around it. You'll vacuum or mop last. (2) Work in one direction. Move around your room from top to bottom and from right to left. Always start at one end of your home and work toward the opposite end. (3) Listen to music with a fast beat or tune into a talk radio station that you love so you'll have entertainment and motivation while you work. (4) Work in 15-minute increments. You'll accomplish so much, and if you're at all like me, you'll wish that you had more time. (5) Avoid interruptions. Don't answer the phone and don't start tasks that aren't part of your day's plan. (6) Treat yourself for a job well done. A treat is whatever you find truly enjoyable. A good book. Time for yourself. A bubble bath. A movie. Treat yourself for being a speed cleaning pro.

Is the Box Half Full?

How many almost empty boxes of laundry detergent does one need? Or window cleaners? Or bottles of bleach? If your home is like many, you lose so much shelf and cupboard space because you have too many cleaning products and too many partially filled boxes and bottles of liquids. I suggest that you go to the source, pull out all your cleaning products, and put them on the counter. Now go through what you have and consolidate all similar products.

If you need to discard any of them, flush them down the toilet to keep them away from children. Then rinse out the container and set it out with the trash or recycling.

Laughter and tears are both responses to frustration and exhaustion. I myself prefer to laugh, since there is less cleaning up to do afterward.

KURT VONNEGUT

Pleasure is an important component of the quality of life, but by itself it does not bring happiness. Pleasure helps to maintain order, but by itself cannot create a new order in consciousness.

MIHALY CSIKSZENTMIHALYI

Great Gift Ideas

As you prepare for special events that usually bring gifts into your home, make a prearranged announcement that you no longer need any gift that requires shelf space, cleaning, dusting, or handling—you have enough stuff. However, other gifts are useful. Ones that require none of the above are perfect. Movie tickets and gift cards to your favorite restaurant, an upcoming cruise, or a vacation hotel are all especially appreciated.

A few years ago we made an announcement to our friends and family that we didn't want any more stuff, and that we only wanted gift certificates and such. So far, they are sticking with this. At last no more plates, bowls, waffle irons, and glassware. Gradually we have stopped receiving gifts that cause us clutter, and our family has fun surprising us with contributions toward great food, experiences, and entertainment.

When Giving Gifts...

When it comes time for *you* to give a gift to someone, consider giving a gift that doesn't add clutter to that friend's home. Why not give a bouquet of flowers, a box of candy, a bottle of perfume, or a gift certificate for a manicure, a massage, or a facial? Such gifts can be enjoyed for a brief time, but don't take up space in their homes.

So often we forget that others are struggling with the very same clutter problem that we are. Gifts that nurture the body and offer relaxation are such a treasure. I know that some people consider having a bookstore gift certificate in their possession about the happiest thing ever.

When you aren't just buying things, but take time to think through what would bring a smile to a person's face, you end up selecting gifts that are more personal. I guarantee that they will also be well received!

Those Old Trophies...
Dust or Discard?

In 1973 your husband was in a bowling league and his team won several tournaments. At each event your husband was awarded a stunning gold statue with a beautifully engraved plaque that said he was the best. You have looked at those trophies for over 30 years. You've dusted them, picked them up, and moved them to different locations—you're tired of taking care of these old pieces of metal. It's now time to say goodbye to them. (Please, check with your husband first.) This could be true of your children's ribbons and certificates that they received in elementary school (they're now 35-years-old and have been out of your home for 15 years).

What family collections or awards or even past hobby accessories are now taking over your house? Let the pieces go and clear out that space in your house. Another word of advice: Don't hurry to fill that space.

Choose People, Not Things

D on Aslett, a top organizer in America, provides some good advice to help us when we decide to unclutter our homes: "Don't love what can't love you back." Is your first thought, "Well, of course"? Yet think about how much time, attention, care, and yes, even love, we end up giving to our things. We give a lot of ourselves over to selecting a couch. We see an outfit that strikes our fancy and our first words are, "I love this!" We hold on to objects as though our happiness and fulfillment depend on them.

If you can create some distance between your feelings and your possessions, it will be much easier to determine what to keep and what to get rid of. An item that enhanced your life at one point could now be a burden, an obstacle, or a crutch. Spend your time, energy, and love on the people in your life!

New Life for Old Favorites

Don't throw away your favorite mugs or cups just because they're chipped or cracked. Brighten up your kitchen windowsill by planting small plants in those old mugs and displaying them in that sunny spot. Or put that cracked cup near your phone to hold pens and pencils.

Find useful functions for anything that has seen better days. It's surprising how many additional lives an item can have when you get creative. Don't limit your search for an item's new use just to the interior spaces. Your once helpful household item might become a nice accent for your outdoor spaces. Mismatched glasses or vases can become votive candle holders for your patio. Pieces from broken china cups can be used to create a mosaic table top or even stepping stones for the garden. Turn your clutter into new ways to express your creativity.

Pace Yourself

When you're getting rid of all the unnecessary items in your home, pace yourself. I'm not recommending that you start at 8:00 AM and work at it until dinnertime. Once you decide to transform your living space, you might want to tackle it all in a weekend, but you'll better serve your new vision and protect your personal sanity if you take time to create a plan of attack for each area or project.

You can do a lot in 15-minute blocks of time. For every 45 minutes that you work, give yourself a 10-minute break. Change pace, go outside, get some fresh air, walk around the block, get dinner started, vacuum a room—anything to switch gears for a while. When you return and once again focus on de-cluttering that area of your home, you'll feel refreshed and your perspective will be brighter.

Why So Overstuffed?

Storage units are used to hold stuff we don't use. Our homes have run out of space to store our excess. But if you're storing items in an outside storage unit, it means that you aren't using them. Are you paying $300 or more a year storing things that you don't use? If so, you need to evaluate why you have more stuff than can fit into your home. Are you unable to tell yourself "no" when you're out shopping or when a friend asks if you want her stuff? Do you keep everything "just in case" you'll need it later, even if you haven't used it in months? Do you move piles from room to room instead of dealing with what is in those piles? Do you say that someday you'll clean out that garage or the hall closet?

Don't give yourself *more* room to fill. Instead, give yourself more space at home. Take a small step. Maybe one drawer that has always bothered you could be your project for this evening. The progress will feel great, and you can cancel that storage unit because you're well on your way to an uncluttered life.

Cleaning anything involves making something else dirty, but anything can get dirty without something else getting clean.

LAURENCE J. PETER

Good order is the foundation of all things.

EDMUND BURKE, *REFLECTIONS*

Make a Date

Make an appointment with yourself to clean your *(insert project)*. Write the time on your calendar just as though it were a business or doctor's appointment. This will make you keep the date, help you get started, and provide motivation to stick to your plans.

When you put the appointment on your calendar, protect it like you would a top priority. Don't be tempted to cancel it when a better offer comes your way. You don't do that to your friends or to your work commitments, so don't do it to yourself. When you have a project scheduled on an upcoming evening, afternoon, or weekend, spend some time before that appointment considering how you'll tackle it.

Evening Efforts
Ease Morning's Rush

Start your day the night before. Set the breakfast table. Prep the coffeemaker. Create your to-do list for tomorrow. Set out clothes for yourself and the kids. Determine which homework assignments and library books need to go back to school with the kids in the morning and set these near the door. Make school lunches and line them up in the refrigerator. If you're watching your portion control, make yourself a lunch so you won't have to face too many options when you're the hungriest. If you'll need meat for tomorrow's meals, set it in the fridge to thaw. And lastly, set out any items you'll need for tomorrow's projects. If you're painting, get the brushes lined up and the rollers out of the garage. If you're cleaning, be sure all your cleaning supplies are available and handy.

Pray for the day to come and get to bed early. Restful sleep will ensure that tomorrow starts off well and that you'll have energy to handle all that comes your way.

The Idea Jar

I f you can't decide what to do next to make your home better organized, try this. Cut some paper into strips and write down the various projects that need to be done on each of those strips. Place them in a jar—mix them up. When you need to decide what comes next, place your hand in the jar and select one slip of paper. If it reads, "de-clutter the pantry," that's what you do next. When you need another task, go back to the jar and reach in. Bam! You have your next project! As new projects come to mind, write them down on another slip of paper and then drop them into the jar.

The idea jar is great for kids too! Create one that has age-appropriate projects for your children. When it is chore day or the kids are grumbling because there is nothing to do, bring out the jar.

Common Items
Gain Novel Purposes

Repurpose items in your house. A tea cup becomes a lovely little flower container. An old hat transforms into a wall decoration. A bright red vase becomes the perfect accent piece on the mantel. Keep your eyes open. Take something you already have and give it new life and a new purpose.

Here's a clever way to use every smidgen of soap—the bits we save and never know what to do with. Take a square of nylon netting and place a handful of soap slivers in the center. Fold the netting so there are several layers of netting around the slivers and tuck in the ends like a package. Then stitch around all the edges with heavy thread. It's great for scrubbing collar stains or cleaning hands after gardening or painting.

What to Begin With

When you look around and wonder where to begin, understand that the "where" doesn't really matter as much as "what" you choose to begin with. For example, don't start with the garage or kitchen because you will want to complete some smaller projects before you attempt such large and complex areas.

One of the easiest initial projects is the hall closet or the closet near the front door. In a relatively short amount of time, you can have these small spaces done and enjoy that feeling of accomplishment right away.

Next you might choose the room where you spend the most time. De-cluttering that room will give you a sense of control and inspire you to tackle the larger projects.

Time to Get Organized

Back to school time is a great opportunity to get organized. This year plan ahead and make it simpler.

A lot of summer clothing can be packed up and stored in boxes for next summer. Label the boxes according to the clothing size. Then next year pass the clothing along to other family members or friends. There's always a need for perfectly good clothes.

Create a checklist for what you'll need this fall and have your children help—shoes, socks, T-shirts, pants, and uniforms if you use them. Don't forget to list sizes. Knowing what you have will help you shop wisely at those end-of-summer sales. Knowing what you don't need will help you clear out the clutter.

Creative Ways to Make Storage

When storage areas are limited—get creative. In the bathroom, rolled up towels or magazines can be stored in those metal wine racks. Washcloths can be stacked in a wire bike basket that's attached to the wall. In the kitchen, install a shelf about a foot from the ceiling. Use the shelf to store pitchers, punch bowls, and other large, attractive, but seldom-used items. Hang a pegboard in your kitchen to hang utensils and pots. If you have a section of wall space, tack up a series of baskets. These are ideal for holding napkins, coffee supplies, table linens, and even take-out menus.

A refinished old chest of drawers is an attractive way to hold videotapes, DVDs, and CDs. Be creative and in no time you'll come up with some wonderful decorating ideas. You'll also create some great storage spaces!

To live content with small means; to seek elegance rather than luxury, and refinement rather than fashion; to be worthy, not respectable, and wealthy, not rich; to listen to stars and birds, babes and sages, with open heart; to study hard; to think quietly, act frankly, talk gently, await occasions, hurry never; in a word, to let the spiritual, unbidden and unconscious, grow up through the common—this is my symphony.

WILLIAM HENRY CHANNING

Begin a Better Way Today

Sometimes it's hard to start new habits because the old habits have made your home full of clutter.

For example, you may have a box of photographs that date back many years. You know you will never be able to put them all into albums, but what about future pictures? Why not start today by deciding to put all future pictures in albums? Take inventory and see if you already have some albums in a cupboard someplace. You don't want to buy new ones if you already have old ones. Remember, you don't have to put every photograph you take in an album (some may not be of good quality and Uncle Bill really doesn't look good with the top of his head cut off).

Make a new rule: If you can't do anything about the old, you can start today with the new.

Tricks to Tuck
It Out of Sight

One of the first comments women make to me about home management is, "I don't have any space!" That's when you have to work smart! Here are some tips that work for me:

- ☐ Install a towel rack on the inside of the linen closet door to hang tablecloths.

- ☐ Hide storage boxes by stacking them up and placing a plywood round on top. Then cover it all with a pretty cloth. Who will know?

- ☐ Use the tops of cabinets, hutches, and refrigerators to store floral arrangements and baskets.

- ☐ Build a window seat under deep-set windows and use the space for storage.

- ☐ Seldom-used luggage is great for storing out-of-season clothing.

Made in His Image

God is the ultimate organizer. God organized the whole universe to go forward in an orderly fashion.

Do you respond positively to order in your life? I do. I think it is because we are made in the image of God, the One who created order in the universe. That's why you must begin all efforts to transform your life with the heart. Otherwise, the reorganization of house and home will just drive you crazy. But as you open your heart and attitude to God, putting Him first in your life, He will show you little ways to organize the chaos—and lead a more peaceful, ordered existence. It takes time. Be patient. Growing in the spirit is a lifelong process!

Too Many Books?

We build bookshelves to hold books that we only read once. Then we stack those books on that shelf and never touch them again. Sure they are impressive when guests come over, but they usually have limited value to us. Reference books might be an exception, but with easy computer access and powerful search engines, we can research any subject online and find all the information we could ever need.

Consider donating your books to local literacy projects, public libraries, local schools, or adult community centers. You don't have to continue to be the storekeeper any longer. Make room for new books that you are reading.

Sell It

Garage sales and direct sales to customers are two great ways to de-clutter and at the same time make a little money. Place an ad in your local newspaper's classified section. You might say to yourself, "Who would want my old stuff?" You would be surprised at how other people would be glad to buy the things you no longer want or need.

In our area we find consignment stores popping up all over the place. Check with them to see if they might be interested in some of the clothing you no longer use. These stores will make agreements to sell them and give you a percentage of whatever they receive. Often if they aren't able to sell the items within a determined number of days, they will give you the option to come and pick them up or they will donate the items to a worthy cause.

Put Away, Throw Away, or Give Away

Here's a good model to demonstrate how to clean an area. Let's use the hall closet as an example. Take everything out of the closet. Now get focused and toughen up—you need to make good choices about what to do with all the stuff you've just taken out of closet. If you need to, invite a friend over to help you make those decisions.

Now, take a look at the empty closet. Replace only those things that actually belong in a closet—sweaters, coats, umbrellas, tennis rackets, football blankets, and so forth. As for all those items that don't belong in the closet, like papers, photos, magazines, and old clothes, put each item in one of three bags: the Put-Away bag, the Throw-Away bag, or the Give-Away bag. Don't shove any of these things back into the closet. Making final decisions about each item is liberating!

Your Cue to Clean

Give yourself the benefit of cleaning cue cards. Purchase colored 3" x 5" index cards and tabbed dividers. Label the dividers with the following: daily, weekly, monthly, quarterly, biannually, annually, storage. Assign a different color of index card to each section. On the cards, write down jobs that suit each category. For daily chores you might include dishwashing, making the bed, and tidying the house. Weekly chores might include laundry, cleaning the bathroom, and de-cluttering one room. You get the idea.

Here is an example of a weekly chore chart to get you started—adapt it to fit your family's needs.

- ☐ Monday—wash, plan menus
- ☐ Tuesday—iron clothes, water plants
- ☐ Wednesday—mop floors
- ☐ Thursday—vacuum, grocery shop
- ☐ Friday—change bed linens, dust
- ☐ Saturday—yard work
- ☐ Sunday—plan for next week

We seek peace, knowing that peace is the climate of freedom.

DWIGHT D. EISENHOWER

Frugality is one of the most beautiful and joyful words in the English language, and yet one that we are culturally cut off from understanding and enjoying. The consumption society has made us feel that happiness lies in having things, and has failed to teach us the happiness of not having things.

ELISE BOULDING

Monthly and Quarterly Chores

Once you are in the rhythm of taking care of the daily and weekly chores with consistency, it is good to add the monthly and quarterly chores. These will vary from family to family, but there are some basic cleaning needs that most homes require at these intervals. If you've set up the labeled folders and color coded index cards, write these chores on the appropriate cards. Here is a chart to help you form your own.

Monthly Chores

- ☐ Week 1—clean refrigerator
- ☐ Week 2—clean oven
- ☐ Week 3—wax or polish furniture
- ☐ Week 4—clean and dust baseboards

Quarterly Chores

- ☐ Clean windows, cupboards, and closets
- ☐ Move furniture and vacuum

Develop Your Own Style

With a few simple organizing hints, you can find peace in your life! Shoe boxes, cardboard boxes, hat boxes—they're perfect for storing clutter. Plastic bins, stacking trays, and even laundry containers are perfect. Large envelopes are also a great way to organize small items. List the contents on the outside and store the envelopes in one of your boxes. And of course, baskets are perfect for storing arts and crafts for the kids, sewing materials, and gift ribbons and bows.

Over the years people have said to me, "You're so organized!" A few friends think I take it too far...but my systems make my life work more smoothly. We all have to find our own style for life management. When you find your own system, you can live for other purposes! Why waste precious time?

The Annual Paper Purge

The beginning of the year is a great time to go through your file cabinets and discard all those out-of-date papers that are taking up valuable space. You'll be surprised at how many obsolete papers occupy your filing cabinets. They seem to multiply!

When purging, ask yourself why you kept the paper when you first received it. If you don't need it for future use or for tax purposes, get rid of it. Keep tax records and other important financial records in your files for six years.

If you take on this task a couple times a year, you'll be much better off. Just be sure to schedule at least one session at the beginning of the year. Not only will this get your year off to a good, organized start, it will help you arrange information, receipts, and records and make filing your taxes a breeze.

Freedom from Clutter

How much time do you waste because you have so much stuff? If you catch yourself searching for long periods of time and saying "I know I have it here somewhere," you have too much. If you don't know where to find it, then it has no value to you—it's like not having it.

You can't afford clutter. It will deprive you of happiness, emotional stability, and peace. It will rob you physically, emotionally and spiritually. Getting rid of all your clutter will free you up to do more than just housework. With less stuff you'll have more time to do the things you really want to do. For example, you can write that note to a friend. You can write that book, or you can sing in a choir. Freedom from things affords you opportunity to do what you've always wanted to do.

Practical and Creative Solutions

Get practical. If you like to use the mirror over the bathroom sink to put on makeup and fix your hair, but your bathroom has no counter space, make some. Place a large wooden cutting board on top of the sink and you have a place to set your makeup, comb, blow-dryer, and curling iron. The board is easy to remove and store when you are finished with your beauty treatment.

Do you find that you're short on storage for your socks and underwear? If so, try storing them in a hanging shoe bag with clear plastic compartments. The clear plastic pouches let you see what's in them.

Good Reasons to Use Good China

Do you have things in your home that are "too nice to use"? If you can't use something because it's too nice, then those items are taking up valuable space that you could use more efficiently. If you can't use it, then get rid of it. If you can't do that, then start using it.

Begin tonight with dinner. Wouldn't your family be surprised to see you setting the table with the "it's too nice to use" china, linens, and centerpieces? Why wait for special guests or grand events? Your family deserves the joy of a nicely set table!

And when you start using your "best" stuff for the important people in your life, you'll find that the behavior at the dinner table greatly improves. There's a shift in moods and attitudes when your family feels the warmth of special treatment. It will seem like a night out at a fancy restaurant when you serve a plain, basic meal on the fine china. Return to the pleasures of elegant dining at home.

The Must-Have
Junk Drawer

Is there one drawer or cupboard in your kitchen, family room, or maybe in your study where everyone checks for batteries, small screwdrivers and flashlights, seed packets, birthday candles, a letter opener, and matches? Junk drawers seem to appear in every home, no matter how neat the owners are. Rather than banish your designated junk drawer, embrace the idea and organize it.

Silverware sectional containers can help you line up those small tools and pens. Baby food jars or egg cartons are great for keeping screws, hooks, nails, and thumbtacks together and accessible. Junk drawers can become "possibility drawers" when their contents are presented neatly.

Order is the shape upon which beauty depends.

Pearl Buck

*Not merely an absence of noise, Real
Silence begins when a reasonable being
withdraws from the noise in order to find
peace and order in his inner sanctuary.*

Peter Minard

Sorting Laundry
the Easy Way

Laundry! It has to be one of the most time-consuming activities. You can't get away from it because your family will always need clean clothes and bedding.

There are ways, however, to make it an easier chore. Have your little ones help sort laundry into darks, colors, and whites. They'll think it's a game for years before they realize it's an actual chore. If you have a large laundry room or laundry area in your garage, place three different colored plastic tubs by the washer. Label these darks, colors, and whites or have the tub colors reflect these categories. Put a laundry hamper in each child's room and make them responsible for getting their laundry into these bigger tubs. Make it a rule that if it doesn't make it to the tub, it won't get a scrub.

Think Double-Duty

Store extras in your home by thinking of ways certain items can serve double-duty. For example:

- [ ] Store extra blankets by putting them on the guest bed. They are easily removed when you have guests spend the night.
- [ ] Fill rarely used suitcases with off-season clothing.
- [ ] Turn a roasting pan into a catchall for awkward-to-store kitchen gadgets.
- [ ] Arrange small gardening tools in an unused flowerpot.
- [ ] Store some of your extras under the beds.

A Goal for the Whole Family

Make de-cluttering your home a family goal. So often women take on all of the cleaning and organizing chores. Not only does this become overwhelming, it becomes a disservice to the other family members. Everybody who lives in a home should contribute to its balance. When you have a realistic plan that includes age-appropriate chores, you'll reap the rewards of a united, cleaning family.

☐ Three years old: fold and put clothes away, brush hair, make bed, clear meal dishes, and pick up toys.

☐ Five years old: set table, clean bathroom sink, feed pets, walk dog, dust furniture, and help put groceries away.

☐ Seven years old: empty garbage, do schoolwork, clean out car, help make school lunches, and help with meal clean up.

Your Home…
A Lovely Reflection of You

When you can't decide what to toss and what to keep, consider which decorations, dishes, paintings, and pieces of furniture reflect who you are.

I feel immediately at home in houses where people have surrounded themselves with what they love. What do you own that matches your personality and creates the feel you and your family want to communicate? A family photo album, Christmas ornaments handed down from generation to generation (yes, even in the spring!), books, signs, and plaques collected on trips, a verse of Scripture —somehow it all comes together to say *This is who we are. This is what we love.*

The point of it all is to make yourself and other people feel at home. A cluttered dwelling presents mixed messages and will cause unease for visitors and your family. An organized home presents an invitation to stay and enjoy a place that reflects peace, your values, and your style.

Peace—that was the other name for home.

KATHLEEN NORRIS

*Have nothing in your houses that you do not
know to be useful or believe to be beautiful.*

WILLIAM MORRIS

You may obtain seminar information or a price list of materials available by sending your request and a self-addressed, stamped envelope to:

More Hours In My Day
2150 Whitestone Drive
Riverside, CA 92506
www.emiliebarnes.com

Harvest House Books by Bob & Emilie Barnes

Bob & Emilie Barnes

*15-Minute Devotions
for Couples*

101 Ways to Love Your Grandkids

Be My Refuge, Lord

*A Little Book of Manners
for Boys*

*Minute Meditations
for Couples*

Bob Barnes

*15 Minutes Alone
with God for Men*

*500 Handy Hints for
Every Husband*

Men Under Construction

*What Makes a Man
Feel Loved*

Emilie Barnes

The 15-Minute Organizer

15 Minutes Alone with God

*15 Minutes of Peace
with God*

*15 Minutes with God
for Grandma*

*500 Time-Saving Hints
for Women*

Cleaning Up the Clutter

*Emilie's Creative
Home Organizer*

*Everything I Know
I Learned in My Garden*

*Everything I Know
I Learned over Tea*

Friendship Teas to Go

Garden Moment Getaways

A Grandma Is a Gift from God

Heal My Heart, Lord

Home Warming

If Teacups Could Talk

I Need Your Strength, Lord

An Invitation to Tea

Join Me for Tea

A Journey Through Cancer

*Keep It Simple
for Busy Women*

Let's Have a Tea Party!

A Little Book of Manners

A Little Hero in the Making

A Little Princess in the Making

The Little Teacup that Talked

Meet Me Where I Am, Lord

*Minute Meditations for Healing
and Hope*

More Faith in My Day

More Hours in My Day

*Quiet Moments for
a Busy Mom's Soul*

A Quiet Refuge

Safe in the Father's Hands

*Simple Secrets to
a Beautiful Home*

Survival for Busy Moms

A Tea to Comfort Your Soul

*The Twelve Teas®
of Celebration*

*The Twelve Teas®
of Friendship*

The Twelve Teas® of Inspiration

What Makes a Woman Feel Loved